School Environment Sensory Checklist

Creating Optimal Learning Environments for ALL Children

Deb Hopper

www.lifeskills4kids.com.au

School Environment Sensory Checklist: Creating Optimal Learning Environments for ALL Children

First Published in 2017 by Deb Hopper
Life Skills 4 Kids.
PO Box 210, Forster, NSW 2428 Australia.

©2017 Deb Hopper/ Debbie Hopper
The moral rights of the author have been asserted.

National Library of Australia Cataloguing-in-Publication entry.
ISBN: 9780994448323 (print)

Subjects: School environment - Psychological aspects.
Study environment.
Education.

Dewey Number: 370.158

Cover and internal design by Nelia Olival
Book production by Life Skills 4 Kids
Printing in Australia by Ingram Spark

DISCLAIMER

ACKNOWLEDGEMENTS

This book could not have been made possible without the generosity of the children and teachers who I have worked with over the past 19 years. Learning how to help children through modifying their learning environments is a life time of learning, and every child and every teacher tutors me to be more observant, problem solve and think more creatively about how even the smallest of changes can make massive improvements for children to learn.

Thank you to my team of Occupational Therapists who have contributed to ideas and editing over the past 2 years. Nadia Loguch, Linda Walters and Sarah Fenn. Thank you for making this resource sharper.

A big thanks goes to schools who have allowed photos of their classrooms to be included in this publication. This includes but is not limited to Manning Adventist School Taree, M.E.T School, Oatlands, Sydney and Border Christian College, Albury.

Thank you for your generosity.

Thank you for purchasing this book. We are very excited to include bonus web resources including a PDF copy of the SESC for easy printing of the checklists.

Scan the QR Code below or use this short link http://qrs.ly/zf5i8te to access the PDF of the book. This will also register you for receiving free life time updates.

"

This is an excellent resource for all teachers, parents and carers, ...in fact anyone who associates with children.

Children have immensely varying needs to perform at their best, and Deb Hopper's detailed checklist and resources have helped us (and others) to tailor our classroom environments and practices to engage our students in ways that enhance their learning. A must read!!

"

Mike Dye (MA)
Principal
Manning Adventist School - Taree NSW

"

The School Environment Sensory Checklist (SESC) is an outstanding resource developed by Deb Hopper and her team at Life Skills 4 Kids. It provides detailed information about sensory processing and how different sensory inputs may affect a child's learning in a classroom environment. Simple strategies are provided to help teachers make accommodations to improve students learning. The resources suggested are easily obtainable and reasonably priced. The five page teacher checklist is clearly laid out and easy for teachers to fill in to help identify the needs of their students. The document is bright, colourful and quick to read, allowing teachers to quickly find the information they need. I would highly recommend that all schools purchase the School Environment Sensory Checklist as it will be a valuable asset to have as part of their resources.

"

Lisa Hughes, Director and Occupational Therapist.
Occupational Therapy Helping Children
www.occupationaltherapy.com.au

School Environment Sensory Checklist

The incidence of developmental disabilities is on the increase, and evidence is showing that up to 14% or 1 in 7 children are struggling with a developmental disability or learning difficulty. In one study, it was shown that there has been a 17% increase over 12 years, largely due to the increase in children with autism, ADHD and other developmental delays (Blumberg, 2012).

In addition, sensory processing disorders affect 5-16% of school-aged chidlren. These children find it difficult to process sensory information and can show a variety of symptoms including hypersensitivity to sound, light and touch, poor fine motor skills and distractibility (Bunim, 2013).

Often, it is the children with learning or developmental difficulties who also struggle with sensory processing. This means that there are often 4 or more children in the classroom who are finding it difficult to cope with noise, light or movement and finding it difficult to cue into learning. The symptoms of either sensory processing or learning difficulties might look like underperformance, behavioural outbursts or opposition, frustration or emotional regulation challenges.

It is imperative that we identify and support children and make sure the underlying reason of WHY they are struggling is understood.

Providing additional support for these children is imposing an increasing challenge for early childhood educators and teachers who are dealing with increased workloads and full classrooms. The School Environment Sensory Checklist (SESC) is a tool that can be used by early childhood educators, teachers, occupational therapists, home school parents, or anyone involved in assisting children's learning. It is a guide to look more closely at the classroom environment and make easy changes which will have big impacts on helping not only the children who are struggling, but all children.

It is really exciting to hear of more research being done on classrooms and how to help children learn through the changing of the physical environment. The Clever Classrooms research from Salford University in 2015 found that well designed primary schools boost children's academic performance and that differences in the physical characteristics of classrooms explain 16% variation in the learning progress over a year! This research found the whole school factors (size, navigation routes, specialist and play facilities) didn't seem as important as the design of the individual classrooms.

The Clever Classrooms report noted that aspects linked to the best level of sensory stimulation for learning should neither be chaotic, nor boring, but somewhere in the middle (Barrett et al, p3).

_____

Barrett, P., Davies, F., Zhang, Y., Barrett, L. (2015) Clever Classrooms: Summary report of the HEAD project (Holistic Evidence and Design). University of Salford Manchester.
Received from https://www.salford.ac.uk/cleverclassrooms/1503-Salford-Uni-Report-DIGITAL.pdf

Blumberg, S. J. (2012) Trends in the Prevalence of Developmental Disabilities in US Children, 1997- 2008. Centres for Disease Control and Prevention for Health Statistics. Presented at National Conference on Health Statistics, Washington DC. August 8, 2012).

Bunim, J. (2013) Breakthrough Study Reveals Biological Basis for Sensory Processing Disorder in Kids. University of California San Franscisco. Cited in https://www.ucsf.edu/news/2013/07/107316/breakthrough-study-reveals-biological-basis-sensory-processing-disorders-kidsi

01 Creating Optimal Learning Environments for Children

Children spend up to 1/4 of their day at schools and in classrooms learning valuable skills for life. It's a highly complex environment, like no other that children interact with. The demands of the classroom learning environment can assist or detract from a child's ability to learn. If a child struggles with learning difficulties, they have a higher probability of having sensory processing difficulties as well, further impeding learning.

The School Environment Sensory Checklist (SESC) has been developed by Deb Hopper, with input from our team of occupational therapists at Life Skills 4 Kids, Australia and in consultation with teachers, learning support staff and independent paediatric occupational therapists. It has been developed and trialed over the past 2 years, and is a useful tool for occupational therapists, teachers and educators to use in the classroom. The checklist is best used in conjunction with the 20 Day Classroom Detox online course.

The 20 Day Classroom Detox, also by Deb Hopper, is another fantastic resource that can fast track your experience and skills. Packing more power, strategies and ideas into the School Environment Sensory Checklist (SESC) will make teaching easier, support your students and make your day easier. For more information on the 20 Day Classroom Detox, see http://www.lifeskills4kids.com.au/are-you-a-teacher/ or link via the QR code below.

Welcome to our School Environment Sensory Checklist guidelines

Here you will find useful information about how various environmental factors can impact and either support or impede children's ability to engage, focus and learn. You will gain an understanding about why it's important to re-examine our schools and classrooms and how changing a few simple things in your classroom will make teaching easier and less demanding.

The checklist at the end of this tool kit will guide you to start creating best practice classroom sensory learning environments. The classroom environment can also impact children's behaviour and ability to self-regulate. With settled and happier students, your teaching will become much easier and their learning will improve.

If you are purchasing this book on Amazon, we highly recommend you download the School Environment Sensory Checklist (SESC) in PDF form to print out and use in your classroom. You can download it by scanning this QR code and entering your details. Download a QR code scanning app on your smart phone. Registering via the QR code below or using this short link (or use this short link http://qrs.ly/zf5i8te) will also ensure you receive updates as this resource is further developed.

02 The Visual Environment

The layout and appearance of your classroom involves several important aspects, such as:

- glare
- light levels and flourescent lighting
- colours
- contrasts
- moving objects.

1. GLARE

Some children and adults have underlying sensitivity to bright lights, fluorescent lights and sunlight. This might occur when looking directly at the light source, filtered light through curtains or blinds, or the reflection off windows, white board or smart board. Be aware of windows or doorways that are untinted, and of brighter times of the day. Glare from windows can reflect onto white boards and smart boards which can be distracting and difficult for some children to look at.

How to reduce glare in classrooms

Reducing glare is generally done by blocking or filtering the light source. This can be done in a variety of ways including:

- Closing the blind across the window or door where the sun is coming in

- Adding a sheet or a curtain across the light source

- Applying for funding to tint windows. This can also reduce heat in hot areas

- Placing posters or art across windows or doors to filter the light (but be careful no to create too much visual busy-ness)

- Placing a large piece of butcher's paper on window and add a visually simple art work to this.

2. FLUORESCENT LIGHTING

The high speed flickering of fluorescent lights and physical responses that our eyes have to very bright light can cause issues for children who may have 'Scotopic Sensitivity', a perceptual processing disorder where the brain has difficulty processing visual information.

Teachers have reported to us that using special light filters (or mood filters) over the standard classroom fluorescents has an overall calming effect on students. It also reduces the incidence of migraine and headaches in affected people.

These light coverings are available under a number of different names, such as mood filters (google them to find your local supplier). They work by blocking out the flickering of the fluorescent lights which can cause visual discomfort or visual stress and can lead to 'behavioural reactions', or more correctly, sensory-driven behaviour. They are specially designed to be safe to use near lights and are constructed from fire safe material. Only use material tested and rated in your state or country as being fire safe and suitable for this use.

3. VISUAL BUSY-NESS OR VISUAL CLUTTER

The visual 'busy-ness' of a classroom also has a stimulatory effect on some children who may be over-responsive to lots of competing visual information such as too much colour or patterns on display, too many overlapping objects or pictures on the walls, high colour contrast pictures and wall paint that is too bright or has strong visual patterns.

Having too many beautiful works that students have created in the class (particularly hanging objects and pictures) can also serve as visual distractions for children who lack the underlying abilities to filter out the visual information they don't need to be focusing on. Simpler visual displays on walls as shown here can help reduce this feeling of visual clutter.

One really effective tip is to use 'visual blocking'. This is where craft or posters are 'blocked' together on a simple solid color background. Visual 'blocking' can also mask the 'busy' lines on a brick wall, making them less distracting.

With a creative and mindful eye, it is possible to strike a balance between visual overload and the need to display children's beautiful crafts and creations.

The Auditory Environment

While most people with a mature auditory nervous system can tune out irrelevant noises and chatter, children who have persistent difficulty with focusing and listening may actually be struggling to tune out irrelevant noises and chatter on a neurological level.

For children with a Central Auditory Processing Disorder, or with specific difficulties in certain areas of auditory processing ('listening' and 'understanding', not just hearing), even the most organised classroom can pose challenges for a child to process and filter auditory information.

Clocks ticking, pencils scratching, people talking outside or cars driving past the school are noises that can trigger a stress response in people with auditory difficulties, or distract them from the task they are trying to focus on.

As they get older, most children develop cognitive strategies to cope with some of these triggers. But for some children it is just too much. Even by teaching cognitive strategies some children may not make the connection between the noise and their levels of stress or stress behaviour responses. After all, this is normal for them; they have never experienced the world differently.

Some children have auditory processing difficulties and struggle to process speech in the presence of background noise. It is important to consider where these children sit, how far away they are from the speaker, or how close they are to competing noises like fish tanks, windows and distracting chatter.

Some strategies for helping a child cope with noise includes:

- rearranging seating slightly

- providing noise-cancelling headphones

- allowing the child the opportunity to have a quick break out of the classroom for relief from the background noise of the classroom.

For some children, once they reach their threshold or tolerance level for noise, they are unable to tell a teacher that they have had enough auditory input. A child may communicate this through an emotional outburst, by running out of the classroom, distracting other children, or being disruptive in class. It is like they have reached their limit of coping and once this happens, they react from a stress fight or flight response.

Being aware of the noise levels in classrooms and strategies to reduce noise producers can make a significant difference to children who struggle with auditory processing or auditory figure ground difficulties. As adults, we have the capacity to screen out auditory distractions or regular auditory producers, such as the sound of children pulling out their chairs from their desks, sharpening their pencils, moving of papers on their desks, the sound of a pencil writing or chatting to a friend in group work time. However, for many children, these auditory distractions are hard to screen out and it may be very tiring for them to keep tuned into and persevere with listening while screening out background noise.

Many of these classroom noises are unavoidable and are a part of classroom daily life. The use of soft furnishings, posters, carpet on floors and carpet - like lining on walls as poster boards, even paper posters, can assist in buffering and reducing the overall noise levels within the classroom. Using rubber feet on chairs and tables can assist in reducing general classroom noise.

The Tactile / Touch Environment 04

Classrooms (especially in the younger years) can be wonderfully messy, explorative places with a wealth of tactile information. For many children, playing with paint, water or plant materials is the highlight of the school day.

THE 'TOUCH' AVOIDER

However, for the child with touch or tactile sensitivity, (that is, difficulty processing tactile information), these messy materials can cause a distressing physical response. Any kind of feedback, perception or registration through the touch sense (registered through our skin) can cause discomfort, pain or fear, leading to an avoidance or withdrawal response. Put yourself in the shoes of a young person with such avoidance responses and imagine how 'on guard' they must feel during the day in the presence of so many people moving about, who may brush up against or bump in to them, such as when they are lining up to go into class.

Just as some children struggle to identify their auditory issues because they have never known anything different, so it can be difficult for touch sensitive children to articulate their fear and stress. It is particularly difficult for children when they are getting in trouble for having melt downs, reacting or acting out 'for no apparent reason'. But is may be that another child has just walked near them or bumped them accidentally on the playground, and their nervous system has misinterpreted this as being the other child hitting them. Understanding and finding out "why" this is happening is the first step in really helping a child and their teacher to make accommodations or change the environment. Strategies may be put into place to change the way they are encouraged to interact at class line up (such as being first or last in line), or other times when they need to interact with tactile media such as paint or glue.

Being on the edge of this fight or flight response all day due to the ongoing 'threat' of uncontrollable touch input takes its toll on the nervous system, and produces very real stress responses that have a similar impact to any fear or phobia on long term health and mental wellbeing.

Deep touch pressure, firm massage and movement breaks that engage the large muscles of the body can have a protective effect on reducing touch sensitivity.

Some strategies that can be used in class or on the playground to help with children who find it difficult to deal with touch include:

- Allowing children to play on the fixed/ climbing equipment before art time (to gain muscle input, which is calming and organising)
- Doing wall push ups or desk push ups in class to help calm them
- Encouraging the child to give themselves a firm hand massage before touching glue or paint
- Giving themselves a big hug can be a helpful and easy self-calming tool.

THE 'TOUCH' SEEKER

Many children seek out touch input in class. These are the children who fidget and find it difficult to keep their fingers and hands to themselves. They fidget because their nervous systems are seeking and craving touch / tactile sensory input. By allowing them to fidget and move, they are actually able to more easily concentrate and therefore engage and learn.

Strategies in class for those with fidgety fingers include:

- Having a box of fidget toys or hand fidgets available at story time from which they can choose one to play with. This may include a box of different types of balls or stress fidgets, different textures of material, nuts and bolts to fidget with or sand paper to touch and feel. There are many different options available from sensory shops or your local bargain shop or supermarket
- Encouraging a child who fidgets to sit close to you at the front so you can encourage them to be a part of the story and help you turn the pages
- Playing finger games or doing finger stories regularly
- Seating a child who fidgets away from a child who is touch over-sensitive so they don't increase the other child's stress response
- Doing some seat pushups on the floor before the story (muscle input) which will help to decrease fidgetiness.

Google fidget toys or fidget balls to find your closest stockist.

Seating Options for Fidgety Children

Many children struggle with low muscle tone and poor postural control. This makes it difficult for them to 'sit up', 'sit still' or sit for long periods. Many children benefit from using different options for seating such as:

- move n sit cushions
- core disc cushions
- disco sit cushions
- hokki stools
- ball chairs / chair balls

or other seating options to ensure their comfort so they can concentrate in class.

Move n sit cushions - a tried and true seating favourite

So how do these seating options assist in concentration or attention?

When we give the nervous system movement input (which is what happens when we sit on one of these cushions, balls or stools) our balance or vestibular system is stimulated. Once we feed the vestibular system, it allows us to concentrate better and for longer.

06 Movement Options in Class and at School

Our bodies are designed to move, and research shows that our nervous systems need movement input to enable us to learn.

OUTSIDE MOVEMENT

Having playground time before school starts is an easy way to get children's nervous systems ready to learn. Often the challenges at schools is that children need to be monitored by a teacher when accessing playground equipment. Safety is paramount, but with teacher demands and increased workloads many schools aren't able to offer playground supervision before school due to current staff protocols or rosters.

It is a shame that many playgrounds and fixed equipment areas are closed to students before school, which is the best time for them to play and stimulate their sensory systems ready for school. A child needs movement BEFORE they learn. Perhaps this is a challenge to increase awareness to school teachers, school administration and school boards to change the culture and increase the awareness and importance of letting children experience movement and muscle (e.g. climbing) time before the school day starts.

CLASS MOVEMENT

Some children need movement while they are seated at their desk for optimal learning and concentration. Ball chairs can improve fine motor skills when children sit on them at their desk. Leaning onto ball chairs or small exercise balls at floor time can also help children to stay alert and attentive. Ball chairs come in all sizes from 45cm for preschoolers to 75cm for tall adults. They have little 'feet' at the bottom so they don't roll away and can be placed on the desk for cleaners. Very smart, and they make kids even smarter! Google ball chair or chair ball for your local online shop or stockist.

Having some exercise band / physio band around the bottom of a chair can also allow children with fidgety legs to push and pull against the band, which increases concentration and attention.

Playground and Outside Equipment

> *We must perceive in order to move, but we must also move in order to perceive*
>
> J.J. Gibson

Children need to move BEFORE they are able to learn. Researchers have found that in children with ADHD, when they were moving the most, the majority performed better in tasks of working memory, and that they only started moving when they were working on complex cognitive tasks (Sarver et al, 2015) .

However, most playgrounds in our schools consist of fixed climbing equipment. Some have flying foxes or zip flyers, but in our experience, these are often taken away or restricted for fear of injury.

For lack of supervision, or for safety reasons, children are often not allowed to use fixed or climbing equipment before school, which is when they would really benefit from it the most - before key learning times.

Having a solid understanding of children's sensory needs and understanding the importance that giving children opportunities to climb, swing, jump and move before learning activities will lead schools and early learning centres to highlight the importance of including more 'movement-based' playground equipment.

Sarver, D.E., Rapport, M.D., Kofler, M.J. et al. J Abnorm Child Psychol (2015) 43: 1219. doi:10.1007/s10802-015-0011-1

WE OWE IT TO OUR STUDENTS TO PROVIDE MOVEMENT SOLUTIONS IN SCHOOL PLAYGROUNDS.

Below are some examples of playground equipment that can be safe and provide movement sensory input for students.

This rope swing is great as it allows movement forwards and backwards and from side to side.

It can be used for all ages, but is great for older children too. It doesn't look like a swing, but is still fun and allows for needed movement. It can also be used for climbing and provides awesome muscle (proprioceptive) input.

This hammock allows for swinging next to friends, or one child can receive some lovely deep touch pressure input while lying and being swung in a gentle arc. Or for sensory seekers, it could be used as a fast and high swing to have fun with friends.

As you complete the checklist, think creatively how you can promote and improve access to movement activities in your playgrounds.

School Environment Sensory Checklist (SESC)

Deb Hopper (Copyright 2017)

Maximise the benefits of the School Environment Sensory Checklist (SESC)

1. If you purchased the Kindle version from Amazon, register here to receive a free copy of the printable PDF for easy printing. This will also register you for free life time updates.

2. If you have already received the PDF, register here for free lifetime updates.
   (or use this short link http://qrs.ly/zf5i8te)

3. The School Environment Sensory Checklist is an invaluable tool for individual classroom teachers, occupational therapists and other health professionals. But why stop at one classroom? Encourage your whole team to join you and you could transform an entire school!

Get on board, have more fun and create massive change for students' learning!

Join together and transform a whole school!

School Environment
Sensory Checklist (SESC)
Deb Hopper (Copyright 2017)

Visual	Yes	No	Action Needed (If Required)
Does the classroom have lots of windows that allow natural light in to the room?			
Does the classroom have windows that face out to a busy area/road/playground/hallway etc where there may be lots of movement?			
Does the classroom have fluorescent lighting?			
Are any fluorescent bulbs flickering? Do any need replacing?			
Does the classroom have light/mood filters over fluorescent lighting? Are they needed to reduce any flickering?			
Are there more than two tones/paint colours on the wall? What colours are they? _____			
Are the colours distracting or calming? _____			
Are the classroom desks/chairs/floors very brightly coloured? Please make notes about the colour of the following 1. Desks _____ 2. Chairs_____ 3. Floors/carpets _____			Are colours complementary? Yes ☐ No ☐ Do colours clash? Yes ☐ No ☐
Is there more than 1 wall covered in classwork/projects/pictures?			
Is there colour blocking over any brick walls?			
Is there colour blocking to group like art/craft/paintings/visuals or routines together?			
Is there more than 1 row of hanging classwork/projects/pictures attached to the ceiling?			
Would you describe the classroom as generally busy or cluttered in appearance?			

Visual	Yes	No	Action Needed (If Required)
Do the hanging classwork/projects/pictures block the line of sight for teacher or students?			
Do the desks face toward the board/primary teaching area? What are the pros and cons? Is this working?			
Do the desks face toward each other so that students work collaboratively? What are the pros and cons?			
Do children with learning difficulties seated in group seating for collaboration need to sit straight on to see the board without turning?			
If yes to the above, are there more than 4 students in these groups?			
Other Comments			

Auditory	Yes	No	Action Needed (If Required)
Is the classroom very large and/or potentially prone to echo?			
Is the classroom very small or narrow/angular in shape?			
Does a speaker have to speak loudly in order to be heard clearly from one end of the room to the other?			
Does the teacher mainly speak in middle of classroom? Does this make listening easier or more difficult for some students?			
Does the teacher's voice project clearly to back of classroom?			
Does the teacher mainly speak at the side of the classroom?			
(Please note that when a teacher speaks to the side of students it may be more difficult for them to understand or some children may need longer to process auditory information)			
Are there any students in the class who may speak loudly on a regular basis? Does this distract other children?			
Are there times during the day where children break off into groups or pairs to complete group work or to discuss? What is the noise level during group time?			
Does the whole class generally have difficulty transitioning from lunch/break times, group work etc into quiet or desk work?			

Auditory	Yes	No	Action Needed (If Required)
Does the teacher tend to speak in a very loud or very soft voice? Loud/soft			
Does the teacher tend to speak in a very high or low pitched voice? High/Low			
Does the teacher have a distinct accent different to the majority of children in the class? This may make listening and understanding more difficult for children of different nationalities.			
Are there any other factors outside the class which may provide background noise? eg refrigeration units, air conditioning, open or conjoined classrooms, roads, canteen, offices, main hallways etc.			
Other Comments			

Tactile	Yes	No	Action Needed (If Required)
During art and craft activities, are there opportunities for children to regularly and discretely avoid messy surfaces/textures/substances? Would it be easy to miss observing children who avoid touching sticky glue or paint who may be over sensitive to touch?			
Are messy surfaces/textures/substances regularly provided during free play opportunities?			
Are fidget toys trialed and available for students, or any other products/solutions such as physio band under chairs, physio band as a fidget toy, blu-tack?			
Other Comments			

Seating options	Yes	No	Action Needed (If Required)
Are alternative seating options provided for students if required? eg move and sit cushions, ball chairs, hokki stools?			
Can all children's feet touch the floor when seated?			
Is a child's elbow at approximately 90 degrees to the table when seated with feet on floor or supported?			

Movement / Muscle Breaks	Yes	No	Action Needed (If Required)
Are students often encouraged to play using physical contact? eg chasing games, pair exercises, climbing?			
Does the available outdoor fixed equipment utilise multiple planes of movement (front and back, side to side, spinning, upside down)?			
Is the playground/fixed equipment available to students before school and in all breaks eg recess and lunch?			
Are movement breaks incorporated into classroom scheduling? If so, please indicate frequency and duration:_____			
Other Comments			
Some movement strategies I can incorporate into class include:			

Tools for the Mouth	Yes	No	Action Needed (If Required)
Is this a crunch and sip school?*			
Are drink bottles allowed to be on desk for regular sipping and mouth input? This can aid in hydration and mouth input to increase concentration.			
Is chewing gum allowed for those children who need this?			
Are mouth activities included in the school program eg blowing and sucking through a straw to pick up cotton wool balls for maths activities?			
Other Comments			

* Crunch and sip is a friuit or vegetable break in class in Australian Schools. It is a great way to promote healthy nutrition, but it is also great as a sensroy tool which helps children stay alert and focused on task.

We would love your feedback to continue to improve the School Environment Sensory Checklist (SESC).

Please email SESC@lifeskills4kids.com.au to provide feedback and ideas for more items.

Playground and Outside Equipment	Yes	No	Action Needed (If Required)
What challenges does the outside playground equipment give children's sensory systems? Does it provide the following sensory input?			
• Movement – forward and back eg swings, flying fox, zip slider, slippery dip/slide			
• Movement – up and down eg trampoline, see-saw or teeter totter			
• Movement – spinning			
• Muscle – eg climbing, monkey bars			
• Balance activities eg balance beam, balance on edge of curb			
• Deep touch pressure eg crash mats/impact mats			
Other Comments			

3 great incentives to implement changes you identified using the School Environment Sensory Checklist:

1 Boost your students' engagement, focus and academic performance

2 Support ALL your students by reducing the impact of environmental factors that cause sensory overload

3 Spend more time teaching and less time dealing with stressful distractions

Action Notes

Action Notes

www.ingramcontent.com/pod-product-compliance
Lightning Source LLC
Chambersburg PA
CBHW080902030426
42336CB00017B/2984